D1090714

the nature of dwellings the architecture of david hovey

the **nature** of **dwellings**   the architecture of david hovey

Edited by Cheryl Kent

RIZZOLI
NEW YORK

This book is dedicated to Eileen, David Jr., Tara, and Lauren.

First published in the United States of America in 2004 by
Rizzoli International Publications, Inc.
300 Park Avenue South
New York, NY 10010
www.rizzoliusa.com

ISBN: 0-8478-2645-7
LCCN: 2004092965

© 2004 David Hovey
Photographs © 2004 Bill Timmerman, Bill Timmerman Photography
except
© Hedrich Blessing: Bob Harr: 187; Bill Hedrich: 154–59, 163–71,
175–79, 183; Jim Hedrich: 8; Nick Merrick: 4, 7, 94, 96, 100,
111–15, 120; Scott McDonald: 182, 188, 189–97; Jon Miller: 7, 13,
123, 124, 126, 128, 131, 135–37, 140, 144–47, 150, 152, 153,
184, 186, 199, 202–205; Jeff Millies: 206
© GA Houses, Yoshio Takase: 10, 160, 162, 173, 174, 180
© David Hovey: 161
© Tim Lanterman, Tim Lanterman Photography Inc.: 208
© Dino Tonn, Dino Tonn Photography Inc.: 104, 105

"A Machined Model of Affordable Design" © 2004 Cheryl Kent

All rights reserved. No part of this publication
may be reproduced, stored in a retrieval system, or transmitted
in any form or by any means, electronic, mechanical,
photocopying, recording, or otherwise, without prior consent
of the publisher.

Designed by Jensen & Wilcoxon, Inc., Minneapolis
Printed in China

2004 2005 2006 2007 2008 / 10 9 8 7 6 5 4 3 2 1

david hovey: architect, developer, contractor

Ron Krueck

To appreciate David Hovey's architecture—the rigorous thought that goes into it and the architectural freedoms it embraces—it is necessary to know something about the architectural atmosphere in which Hovey was trained. That environment allowed Hovey to integrate fundamentals of architecture together with new approaches so that he could create a new architecture in the Modernist doctrine.

David Hovey's architecture began with his studies at the Illinois Institute of Technology (IIT) in the 1960s. As director, Ludwig Mies van der Rohe had developed a highly structured program that continued to evolve from 1938, when he arrived, until he left in 1957. It was this reflective program that colored the world of his students throughout their lives. During the time Hovey attended, IIT followed the model developed by Mies. In the hands of his direct architectural descendants, the program proved to be resilient; its fundamentals were not challenged by his heirs. This circumstance was simultaneously strength and weakness—the strength in maintaining Mies's vision; the weakness in devolving into an

academy, where learning became repetitious. The professors lost sight of the fact that a part of Mies's educational practice was to question and to look for the freedoms within the intellectual boundaries he set. Fortunately, a few exceptional professors did look for freedoms within this academic atmosphere. Hovey learned from both groups, and in doing so, he both defined the underpinnings of his architecture and liberated his vision. Respect for structure, materials, and their expression; clarity and the movement through space; the efficiencies of planning; the integration of color, line, and texture—these were the program fundamentals Hovey easily integrated into his architecture. Investigating the unknown, applying powers of contemplation and resolve were the alternate requirements his mentor and thesis advisor, Arthur Takeuchi, demanded. These combined investigations led Hovey into a new world of architecture.

While Mies's architecture ostensibly embraced the machine, his aesthetics were dependent on the elegance of a handcrafted finish. Hovey's thesis would demonstrate a way to truly embrace the machine through the development of a prefabricated architecture. The machine would be the essence of the work and, unlike earlier architects, Hovey would take advantage of its efficiencies and

Opposite:
David Hovey on the stairs of Ravine Bluff.

Entrance to Sheridan Elm.

celebrate the aesthetics of the process. Hovey's thesis work seemed to acknowledge Mies's great architecture and to suggest that another Barcelona Pavilion or Seagram Building could never be built. Instead, the great tradition was now in the hands of a young architect, David Hovey, who understood and respected it, and who knew how to allow it to evolve and be vital.

Elaborating on his studies at IIT, Hovey looked at the role that art could play in the definition of space and the relationships that could be developed between objects. He worked briefly with James Speyer, curator of twentieth-century art at the Art Institute of Chicago, who had been Mies's first graduate student and had served on his faculty. In developing a series of exhibition spaces and installations for Speyer, Hovey was exposed to a wealth of contemporary visual arts, the knowledge of which would continue to serve him in his later work. Subsequently, Hovey worked in Takeuchi's office for four years and then went on to work with Helmut Jahn at C.F. Murphy (now Murphy/Jahn). There he experienced, for the first time, one of the most refined design processes of any architecture practice in America.

After four years with Jahn, Hovey decided to open his own office, intending to integrate the knowledge he had gained with a professional structure that suited his personality. Hovey was inpatient and wanted to build. He also wanted complete control; he could not wait for, nor be at the whim of, any client. His office would be organized unconventionally, serving at once as client-developer, architect, contractor, and seller of his

buildings. This innovative method, which bypassed the "Yield" and "Stop" signs, was defined by its name: "Optima."
Any one of the roles Optima took on is difficult to play successfully. Historically, these roles have been separated by a system of checks and balances on building projects. By removing these conventional barriers and taking on greater responsibilities, Hovey was in a unique position to streamline the building process, and he was in a position to allow his architectural vision to flourish.

Optima is a success, and its structure has allowed Hovey to build quickly, to create stronger architecture as he controls the risks and rewards of development and contracting to architecture's advantage. Architecture remained first in Hovey's equation, and that is what makes Optima unique. Optima builds Hovey's visions of a machined architecture in which economics become the means and efficiency determines the methods of construction, establishing a near-prefabricated technique. As these positions evolved, they reinforced Hovey's endeavors; the success of each project allowed him to build stronger works. The mandates of Modernist architecture could now be amplified since the client, the architect, and contractor were all striving for the same vision.

The Work

Hovey's intuitive ability is apparent in his masterful drawings, which illustrate his understanding of the greater implications of the third dimension. He works with layered, almost collagelike spaces, creating an architecture that allows planes to float peacefully, or to collide, in response to spatial pressures. The structure is developed as the most delicate infinite grid that, at first, holds the composition together. Later, the structure will be developed as an integrated part of the composition. This is not a new architecture; it is referential to Mies's Museum for a Small City. In Hovey's hands, however, it is individualistic. His sense of abstraction is difficult to create and maintain in the built world. It insists that architectural elements be defined by edges that dematerialize, releasing them from gravity, as columns become lines in space, and as walls become planes of varying densities embracing and modulating spaces. The final resolution of the components must become one, that is, an integrated whole, a complete work of architecture, where all parts establish their appropriate weights within the composition. This abstraction is what allows certain works of architecture to enter a spiritual world demanding new readings as viewers transverse the space.

It is remarkable to look at Hovey's portfolio with Optima as it unfolds. The first work is a firm rectangular masonry block of town houses on the south side of Chicago whose refined proportions and punched openings recall Mies's early masonry houses. Because of Hovey's fascination with steel, the portfolio quickly turns to his first lean steel and glass house in Sheridan-Elm. Its girded structure and taut enclosure define a delicate

Sterling Ridge.

Fireplace at Sterling Ridge.

mass that is liberated by extending walls into the garden. Its energy is therefore released, as it takes full advantage of the confined rectangular site in an affluent suburb north of Chicago. At this point, Hovey's work can be directly related to the layered space of Mies's courtyard studies. The space is flattened and collaged with color liberally applied. Unlike Mies, Hovey has accepted simplified detailing. The aesthetics of the modular Sandy Knoll house are not dissimilar to those of Sheridan-Elm, although the section fractures at Sandy Knoll in order to conform to the ravine site where the house is built.

It was in Ravine Bluff, a rugged site with vistas of Lake Michigan, that Hovey's energies were freed. While the pure rectangles can be easily deciphered, they begin to be released from the ground; the edges are pushed and pulled until they are finally broken by a curvilinear deck. Just as the massing has been disrupted, the surfaces of the enclosures are similarly freed, no longer in one plane, as function begins to play its role in defining the depth of the skin. Art is inserted into the house to amplify these freedoms. The aesthetics, as in all of Hovey's work, reinforce one another until all parts are reinforcing the whole. Once a freedom is found, it is developed throughout every dimension of a project, not simply applied.

The greatest change in Hovey's architecture occurred in a series of houses known as the Desert Homes. These are the mature work of a masterful architect. It is here that the collaged aesthetics of space previously developed in plan and elevation are developed in section. Floors are pulled apart, insisting that the contours of

the ground become part of the composition. The roof, no longer a single discrete plane, disintegrates into numerous planes that capture the surrounding landscape and intentionally weave the houses back into the earth. The girded structure demands its integrity, as it continues to add to the abstract qualities of the house. Defying gravity, the structures lift the compositions of the houses above the landscapes that they simultaneously seize. The transparent planes that enclose the houses no longer follow the plan of the pure Modernist rectangle, but fluctuate, dissolving the perception of edge, and further integrating the interior and exterior. These formal moves liberate the Desert Homes from the Modernist architectural doctrines that once stood at the center of Hovey's work. They have not been discarded, but rather have been given a new order.

A work in progress, Hovey's career is a journey, a search for real architectural freedoms. Architects rarely find new readings of space—these have been sought and found by a few artists from Picasso to Stella who work in the freer, boundless world of art—but new expressions of space are firmly established in the Desert Homes of David Hovey.

Opposite:
Ravine Bluff under construction.

sterling ridge

2004
Scottsdale, Arizona

negotiating landscapes

Darren Petrucci and Renata Hejduk

The architect David Hovey is an uncompromising negotiator. Negotiating and working within constraints is familiar to Hovey, who confronts civic restrictions all the time as a housing developer. Unlike most successful developers, he is also an architect who utilizes ingenuity and creativity that provides him with the unique ability to transform a constraint into freedom.

Hovey's most recent residential projects are a series of "case study" houses built at Desert Mountain, a gated community in the northernmost hills of Scottsdale, Arizona. With these houses, the architect mediates between the sublime high Sonoran desert landscape and a desire to continue the architectural language and technological project of Modernism. Here he attempts the resolution of one of Modernism's most difficult negotiations: the mediation between the manmade/technological and natural. It is within a delicate negotiation of these systems that Hovey expresses his desire to find balance between landscape and house.

Sterling Ridge

A narrow road winds through undulating terrain to the top of a hill with a seemingly infinite view to the south. On the site, that view is blocked by the house, which nestles itself within the crook of a deep wash and small hill. At this moment, the student of Frank Lloyd Wright will remember his dictum "No house should ever be on a hill or on anything. It should be of the hill." Other houses in the community do not address the landscape in such a careful and respectful way; they tend to overpower and cut away the low hills covered with desert sage, barrel cacti, and tall anthropomorphic saguaros.

The architectural promenade moves underneath the bridging second floor past a pool of water that passively cools the air. This covered entry court is a compressed and cool space that then pushes out into the open air and southern sunlight to a path across a bridge over a cactus garden. The bridge is supported by marigold-orange steel clear span beams, with a steel handrail painted a bright burnt orange—a dynamic foil to the luminescent green of the paolo brea trees and cacti on either side. The path turns ninety degrees to face the east entrance of the house, acknowledging the spectacular southern view and then meeting the house off axis.

"In the Native American communities in Arizona, each house was a combination of interior space and exterior courtyard, where the courtyard offered shelter from the harsh elements of the desert. I wanted to provide a form of shelter by using outdoor space—not just covered shelter but shelter as defined space from the desert, the animals, the climate."

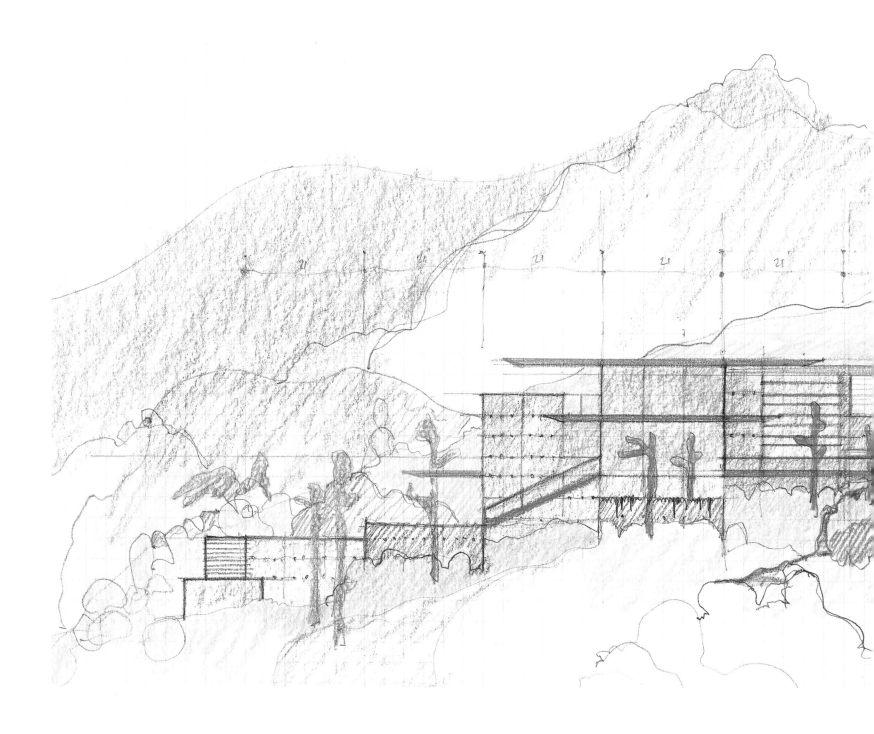

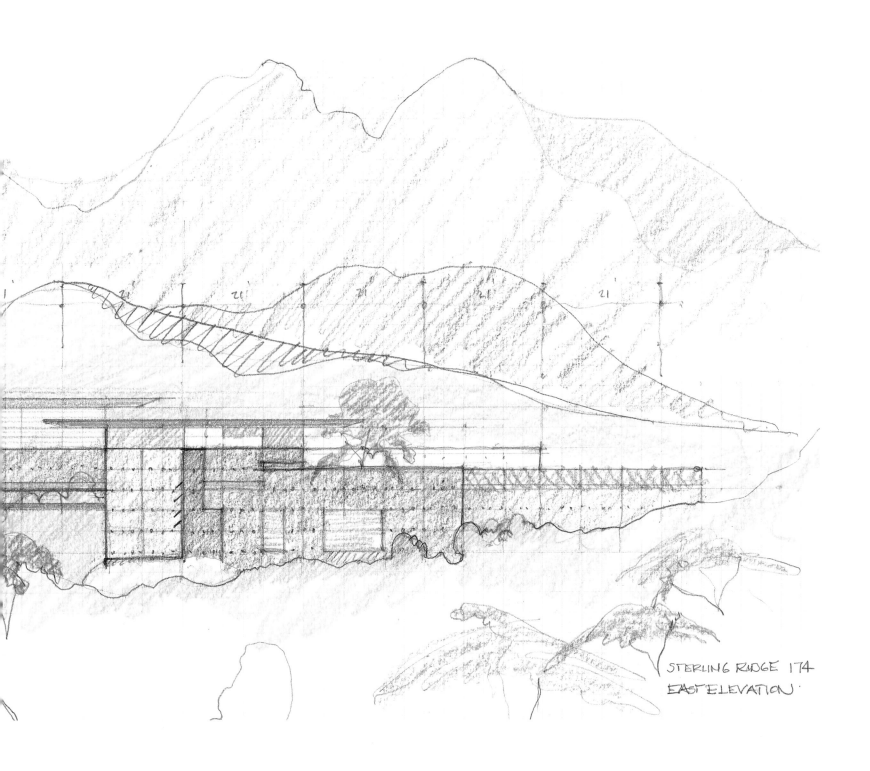

STERLING RIDGE 174
EAST ELEVATION.

Scale

Inside, the scale of the 11,000-square-foot main house is broken down with a series of intimate spaces that are analogous to the exterior sequence of sheltered courtyards. These blur the boundary between interior and exterior and create direct, personal, and human scale relationships to the landscape. Because of the way the house and landscape are terraced gently off the side of the hill, the massing that is broken up by the modulated planes of glass, and the smaller scale courtyards the house is experienced as an assembly of buildings that are layered against the landscape and held together by the rigor of the structural module.

The house is constructed on a 7-foot module with 21-foot bays. The module is the dimensional building block that establishes an economy for the construction and is a proportion conducive to a more open plan. Door openings are six inches wider than usual, for example. At the same time, the rationality and rigor of the module is liberated by the topography and natural systems of the landscape upon which it lies, so that it becomes a filter through which the house surveys the land. In this way, both the house and the landscape are negotiated without compromising the integrity of either. This module never fragments the experience of being inside the house, but instead creates intimate episodes that allow the participants to feel comfortable and rooted within the expansive space.

Although this house does not sublimate itself to the landscape, it has more in common with the work of Wright and his knowledge of Japanese architecture and art than with the heroic villas of the Modernist movement. The house reflects Hovey's understanding of Japanese art, architecture, and landscape design. Through his use of the pictorial device of the layered landscape found in Japanese prints and paintings and that of the borrowed landscape (shakkei) used in Japanese garden design, he incorporates both distant and intimate views of the surrounding environment. Through a precise scalar sequence of layering, he begins on the interior and moves through the house in both plan and section to create an understanding of foreground, middle ground, and background.

Hovey uses his architecture to capture, edit, and frame the intimacy of the immediate landscape and the expanse of the distant view. This strategy is not only employed toward the exterior environment, but is also found within the spatial organization of the interior. Like a good modern house, it is not mimetic of landscape, but it is not in strong opposition to it either. Subtle connections and negotiations create a dwelling that acts as a counterpoint to the wild nature that it holds at bay, while at the same time enhancing and bringing forward the particular nature of existing topography.

Other less formal responses to the natural environment are found in the advanced technological systems in this house. A desire for transparency is antithetic to the extreme heat and light of the desert climate, but Hovey resolves this dichotomy through technical invention. The large floor to ceiling planes of glass combine conventional lamination that incorporates a poly-vinyl butyl inner layer that blocks

99 percent of UV rays with an additional layer of a mylar film impregnated at the atomic level with precious metals that have energy conserving values equivalent to 80 percent of typical one inch insulated glass. These large expansive and transparent walls (protected from the desert sun with overhangs) have none of the visual distortion found in the tempered glass. Thus, the solution both clarifies the view and satisfies climatic and code requirements.

The glass planes of the house are held taught and straight by dusty rose concrete walls. The concrete technology liberates the vertical planes of the house, making possible specific views and relationships with the landscape. For example, long horizontal windows that turn corners without mullions allow the heavy mass of the concrete to appear to float effortlessly over the landscape. This more plastic approach is a foil to the horizontal rigor of the module and reinforces the dialogue with the landscape.

"Although the house is large
and changes in appearance when
seen from different directions,
the fundamental idea is one
of raw simplicity in its composition
of materials and how they are
joined together."

"My intention was to use materials and systems that would work with the character of the terrain. The concrete walls are the same monochromatic color as the desert sand, and the horizontal steel framing is a stronger color found in occasional boulder outcroppings. The greens of the desert vegetation provide contrast."

The concrete is mixed with local sand and cement: its color and texture embody the materiality of the desert floor. The majority of the concrete is distributed on the east and west facades of the house, where its thermal mass absorbs the heat during the day and dissipates it in the cool nights. The concrete becomes as transparent as the glass in its ability to break the boundary between the interior and the exterior.

Water is also used to break down boundaries between house and landscape. The negative edge pool creates a seamless visual connection between the landscape around the house and the desert beyond. Here, this negative edge utilizes the natural evaporation and breezes of the desert to cool the water as it leaves the pool. This exothermic process sends the cooled water through a heat exchanger endothermically absorbing the heated water generated by the building heat pump cooling system. This system allows the swimming pool water to be manipulated to passively regulate or maintain interior temperatures in both the summer and the winter months.

A unique technological and visual innovation is the use of glass solar panels, which are distributed along the south, east, and west perimeter of the upper roof. The 87 panels are directly connected to the power grid, producing 13 kilowatts of energy and offsetting two thirds of peak performance cost of the house. Strategically placed on the roof, these panels shade the space below with a dynamic pattern that animates the facade. Like the other technological innovations, the solar panels have multiple functions: they are both functional and aesthetic.

These passive technologies of solar power, thermal mass, insulation, and exothermic exchange are analogous to the natural processes typically found in the desert environment. Through his innovative use of emergent technologies, Hovey creates a house that survives or sustains itself like a desert plant. Since the early twentieth century, Modernist architects—Albert Frey, Frank Lloyd Wright, Paolo Soleri, Al Beadle, John Lautner, and Judith Chaffee—were drawn to the extreme climate of the desert and absence of restrictions that allowed for experimentation that confronted the boundaries between building and landscape. Today, Hovey's houses extend and advance this experimental and technological research within the constraints of contemporary civic and local covenants, codes, and restrictions. Not only is he contributing to the advancement of the project of architecture, but he is also liberating the boundaries between the built form and the extreme environment whether they are natural or civic. The significance of this negotiation is concealed by the masterful way that the house is designed. From the moment you see the house, you are drawn into its fold and seamlessly begin to engage with the design, programs, and materiality. This ease of engagement belies the significance of what Hovey accomplishes as an uncompromising negotiator.

"As my son discovered during his research for a master of architecture thesis, the use of solar panels to create electricity was particularly suited to Arizona, where there are more than 300 days of sunshine a year. I thought an ideal way to do this was to also use the photo voltaic cells for shading. The resulting textures have been a surprising addition to the richness of the exterior and interior spaces."

"The configuration of the site follows the long axis of the hill with a steep drop at the south end of about 120 feet. The house is approached from the north over a bridge spanning a ravine. Most of the west elevation is dug into the side of the hill while the east is an exposed silhouette with the mountains as a backdrop. The south cantilevers out over rugged boulders."

"Simple rectangular volumes have been stretched vertically and horizontally to create a variety of shapes. They can be viewed from above, from below, from one end to the other. Some are one-story; some are two-story; some are three-story. Interior floors and exterior decks function as mezzanines passing each other in space."

Sterling Ridge upper level plan

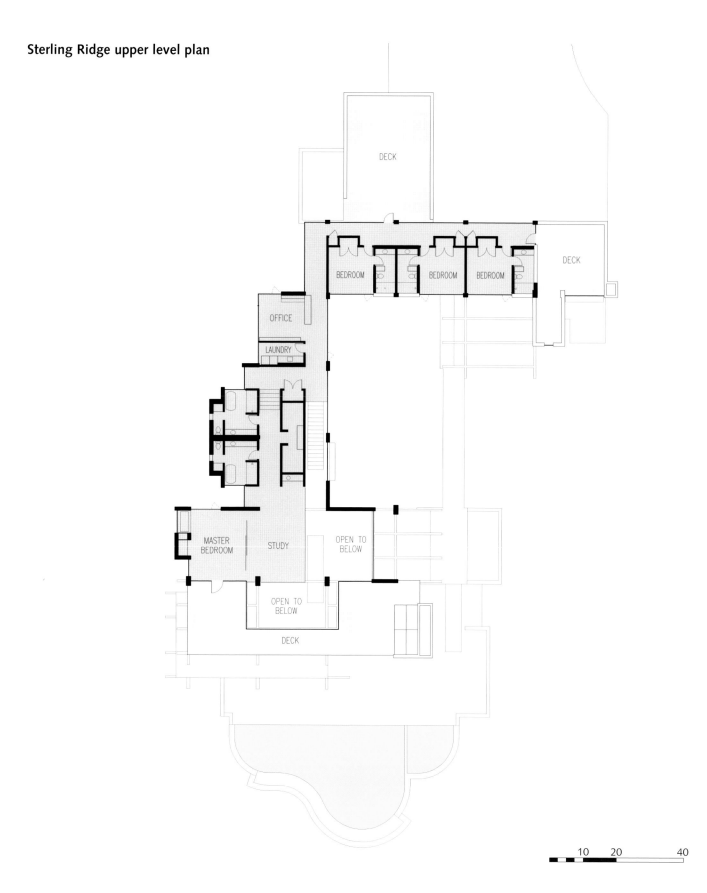

DECK

DECK

BEDROOM

BEDROOM

BEDROOM

DECK

OFFICE

LAUNDRY

MASTER BEDROOM

STUDY

OPEN TO BELOW

OPEN TO BELOW

DECK

10   20   40

Sterling Ridge entry level plan

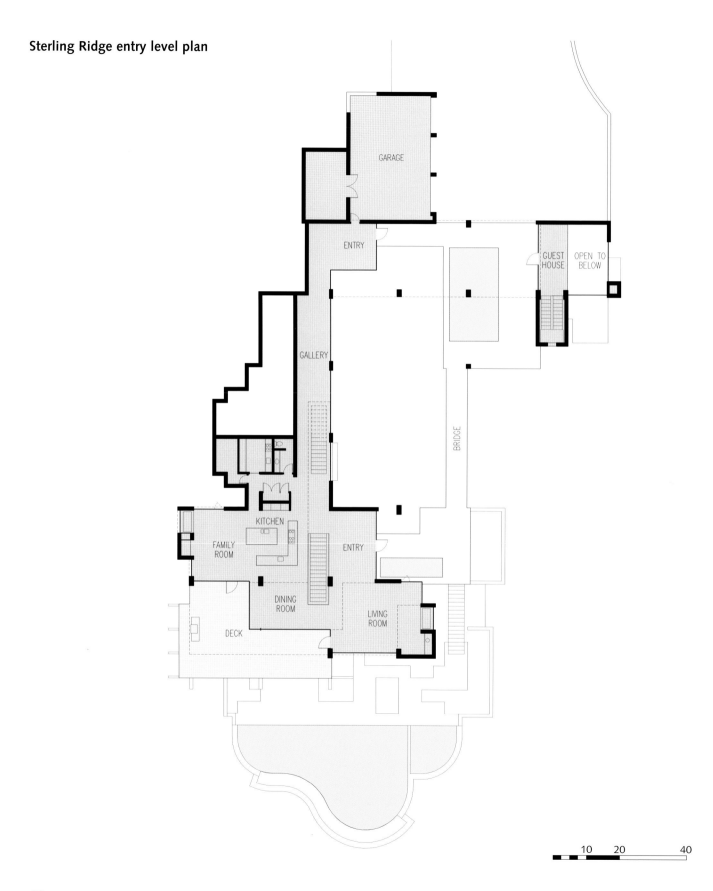

GARAGE

ENTRY

GUEST
HOUSE

OPEN TO
BELOW

GALLERY

BRIDGE

KITCHEN

FAMILY
ROOM

ENTRY

DINING
ROOM

LIVING
ROOM

DECK

10   20   40

Sterling Ridge lower level plan

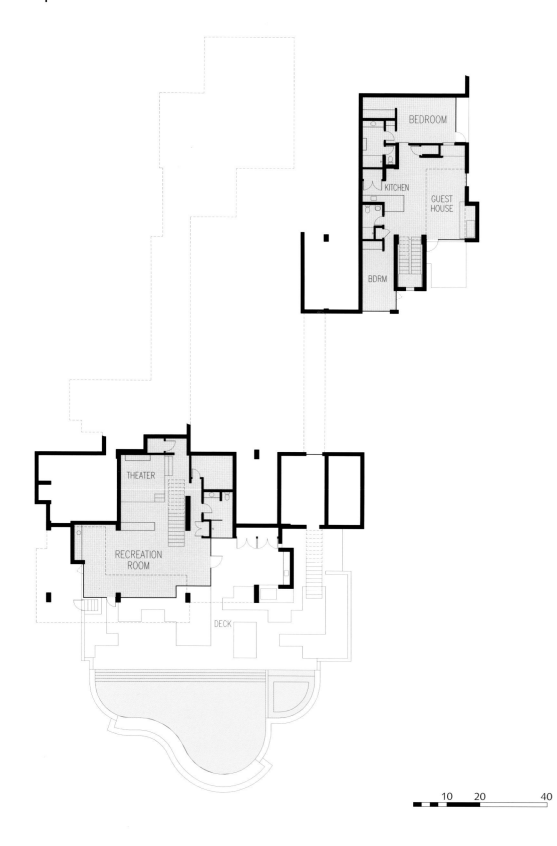

BEDROOM

KITCHEN

GUEST HOUSE

BDRM

THEATER

RECREATION ROOM

DECK

10 20 40

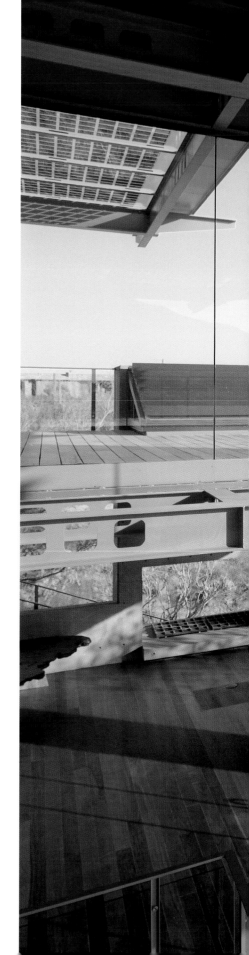

"Sliding translucent panels allow space to change functionally, visually, and emotionally, somewhat like an Alexander Calder mobile sculpture, which continually changes its appearance as its components move silently in the air."

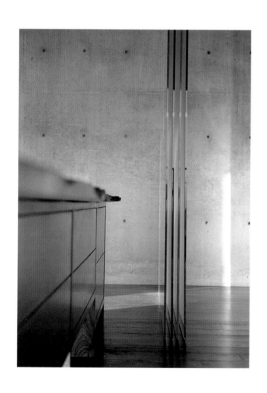

cloud chaser

2003
Scottsdale, Arizona

boundless transparencies

Allison Arieff

Before coming to Arizona in the late 1990s, David Hovey had been searching for a new environment in which to build. He became interested in creating a new type of desert house, and settled in the Saguaro Forest at Desert Mountain in Scottsdale, where everything from the climate to architectural precedents could not have been more different from the environment in and around Chicago. Those differences were just what Hovey was after. He believes good design comes from constraints, and Arizona, with its rugged terrain, arid climate, and Southwestern vernacular tradition, presented challenges that inspired rather than stifled his creativity. In the desert, Hovey was inspired to rethink what a house could be.

His first step was to conceive a new vocabulary for the desert, one far removed from the now-clichéd "Southwest style" associated with the region—he would use no stucco, no adobe. Hovey's approach was influenced in large part by the Modernist tradition. That influence is evident in Cloud Chaser's glass-and-steel structure. Less obvious perhaps is the planning influence of historic Native American homes located three miles from Desert Mountain.

Hovey adapted the Native American concept of the courtyard to the entry at Cloud Chaser. Standing at the crest of a steep ravine, the house is entered through a courtyard at the high point of the site. A path along a dramatic reflecting pool leads to the front door. Inside the entry, one is simultaneously protected from the desert and exposed to its glory. From this vantage point, a panorama of the house interior unfolds as well as an expansive view of Pinnacle Peak, a mountain some ten to fifteen miles away.

An alternate path descends from the courtyard to the lower, terraced level of the house. This zone, accommodating the guesthouse, guest rooms, and recreational areas, is distinct from the upper floor. Where the main level is about expansiveness and distance, the lower level is about containment and proximity. Each level provides a wholly different experience of the landscape. On the lower level, rocks, vegetation, sand, and stone are incorporated in the terrace and all seen up close. Cacti, prickly pears, animals, insects, and reptiles are magnified, as if seen under a microscope.

Apart from mediating views, the courtyard offers protection from the extreme desert climate. While sunlight is a desired and defining factor of desert living, shade

"The idea is to create transparency for views and opacity for protection from the desert heat. The only opaque area on the upper level is the fireplace."

is equally important. And the creation of shade by way of architectural form is essential. The house takes advantage of the sun throughout the day and exploits the physical and psychological benefits of shade. Features like the large overhanging canopies are just one example.

The house's varied roofline follows the surrounding topography. Rather than a single imposing mass, the roof is a series of horizontal planes, a solution dictated by the site and the functional requirements of the building.

Like the renowned mid-twentieth-century Italian architect and engineer Pier Luigi Nervi, who believed architecture and engineering were two parts of a whole, Hovey combines a knowledge of materials and construction to create structures of—to borrow Nervi's phrase—"strength, simplicity, and grace."

At Cloud Chaser, the use of a steel frame creates large, open spaces minimally enclosed with large expanses of glass. Because it lasts forever and will not deteriorate, steel is an ideal structural material for the harsh climate. The framelessly mounted, UV-treated glass provides protection from the elements at the same time that it showcases the natural beauty of the area. Other materials and finishes—including the natural stone and sandblasted colored concrete masonry exterior—were selected to blend unobtrusively into the desert landscape.

For Hovey, it is essential that buildings express on the outside what is happening inside. As little as possible should stand in the way of that relationship. Accordingly, at Cloud Chaser, there is a seamless transparency between the indoors and outdoors. The house expands from its interior and semi-enclosed spaces outward, to the bi-level courtyard and sun deck. Beyond, the negative-edge pool further extends the line of vision.

Elegant bamboo floors and Douglas fir ceilings bring warmth and natural beauty to the interior. The dramatic 63-foot main living room and expansive master suite with sitting room create spacious, inviting environments on the first level.

As the elegant lines and angles of Cloud Chaser attest, Hovey believes in simplicity. But simplicity is not easy. It requires more thought, more perseverance, more tenacity. Hovey aims to create buildings that are sophisticated but simple in terms of construction. His architecture beautifully expresses an economy of means, with elements pared down to what is absolutely necessary.

"The west elevation shows how the
building steps down the site and the
way the roof planes relate to the land.
I chose lavender concrete to pick
up from the myriad of desert colors."

"The wall facing the street starts out at five feet at the entry and rises to thirteen feet as the site slopes down to the south. I wanted to squeeze the entry to emphasize the expansiveness of the courtyard."

"The courtyard is intended to be a
spectacular aesthetic experience,
appealing to the senses in every way.
Depending on the time of day, the
sun changes the mood of the space
from bright and clear to soft,
with beautiful shadowed patterns
in the wall and on the water."

Cloud Chaser entry level plan

GARAGE

COURTYARD

KITCHEN

FAMILY ROOM

TERRACE

ENTRY

DINING ROOM

LIVING ROOM

SITTING

MASTER BEDROOM

TERRACE

Cloud Chaser lower level plan

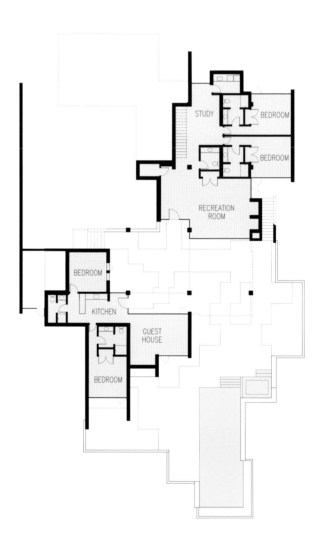

STUDY

BEDROOM

BEDROOM

RECREATION ROOM

BEDROOM

KITCHEN

GUEST HOUSE

BEDROOM

10   20   40

"The house is like Swiss cheese,
with positive and negative spaces.
You can look across, down,
up, inside, and outside. It heightens
your awareness of beautiful and
surprising views."

"I wanted it to feel as though you were standing in the desert when you were in this space. I reduced the construction to the absolute minimum. I let nothing get in the way."

"It was important that the building components be clear. The 7-foot module of the steel structure, the interior wood ceiling, and exterior grating all clearly define boundaries between interior and exterior spaces."

"Here is conception and reality: my perspective drawing and a view looking from the recreation room out to the lower-level outdoor space. Extending the bold horizontal plane creates a protective shady retreat when the summer sun is harsh."

COVERED OUTDOOR SPACE
140 PRELIM.

"I wanted the pool and the water to
make a seamless transition to
the desert, much like the relationship
of the interior to the exterior of
the house."

vanishing rain

2002
Scottsdale, Arizona

"Nearby Native American dwellings
 made of dry-stacked stone
 suggested to me that the building mass
 could be thick and rugged.
 Its texture would be coarse,
 like a magnified view of the trunk
 of Jumping Jolla cactus."

embedding, framing and extending

Darren Petrucci

Vanishing Rain embodies a mature Modernist sensibility and respect for the intense Sonoran Desert climate. In this house, Hovey explores new materials and new spatial relationships with the desert landscape, which can be identified as embedding, framing, and extending. These strategies configure the structure and material composition of the house into a complex set of experiences of the site.

The entry sequence introduces and summarizes the three strategies. The approach begins with a long, gently curved drive surfaced in colored, interlocking concrete pavers that create a tactile transition from the smooth street to the textured stone and wood of the house. The drive culminates in a court framed by three stone elements, the garage to the west, columns supporting a trellis on the south, and a low landscape wall on the east. A wooden footbridge, shaded by a trellis, extends from the house to the court across a pool of water. The bridge is both a symbolic and literal connection between the framed landscape of the exterior entry court and the distant views from the interior of the house.

The house itself is situated over a sloping ridge. With its complex topography and magnificent distant views, the site required a building system that could connect the immediate, more intimate framed

landscape of the ridge with the expansive views of the desert mountains and the city. Hovey used a hybrid building system consisting of a post-and-beam structure supported by a series of load-bearing masses. The heavy masses create an earthbound—or telluric—element grounding the house in its immediate site, while the lighter post-and-beam—or tectonic— system supports a raised, floating platform that connects to distant landscapes. Hovey organized these two systems using the Modernist planning device of a building module. The 3-foot, 6-inch module was determined as a synthesis between the structural needs of wood-beam construction, the aesthetics of exposed structure, and the desire for a spatially open and fluid interior. The module also balances the load-bearing walls and column spacing with larger room sizes and uninterrupted glass areas.

All of the load-bearing masses are of precisely laid natural cleft stone. The color and irregularity of the stone connects directly to the natural desert landscape. This integration is most evident where the mass is embedded into the slope of the site, blurring the boundary between the ground and the house. Functionally, these two masses—one on each side of the ridge—enclose the private zone and act as retaining walls. The punched window openings are appropriate to the construction system and, with their modulated light, reinforce a feeling of privacy.

"Since wood is not as strong as steel, post-and-beam construction has inherently more bulk and a different visual expression."

The second landscape relationship created by the bearing-wall massing occurs on the east side of the house. Here the cleft stone wall breaks free from the facade to frame part of the exterior landscape and create a private courtyard. Floor-to-ceiling glass replaces the stone, visually extending the interior out into the landscape. Unlike the constructed plaza landscape of the entry court, this smaller intimate court captures the natural desert landscape as part of the house.

At the southern end of the house, a wide stone column enclosing an exterior fireplace is pulled away from the facade. The freestanding stone mass is carefully placed to pull the eye out of the interior and to frame the covered outdoor living area and second-floor balcony space. By placing an identical element on the interior, Hovey dissolves the boundary between outside and inside, making the house and its surroundings appear as a single, unified landscape.

Hovey is skilled in extending these concepts from the telluric to the tectonic as well. In contrast to the heavy stone massing of the private zone, the public spaces are supported by a lighter wood post-and-beam construction. This frame structure creates a warm material contrast to the stone while permitting the long sheltering cantilevers that shade the glass walls. Reinforcing the ambiguity of the indoor-outdoor relationship, Hovey has used an open plan. The spaces are simply divided by two red-oak furniture units, allowing fluid movement through the house.

The post-and-beam structure enables the house to float over the landscape, capitalizing on the view while simultaneously creating a shaded outdoor living space below. This shading strategy is an ideal solution in the intense heat and light of the desert. In the lower living areas, stained timber beams extend from the interior to the outdoor living areas. This aesthetic continuity based upon the construction module creates the effect of a single living space below and demonstrates Hovey's ability to use structural systems to create complex spatial configurations.

The cooling effect of the covered terrace is enhanced by a water landscape that begins at the entry bridge. This constructed landscape weaves through the house connecting the entry level with the lower level. The sound of the water is soothing and refreshing in the dry heat of the desert, while the light reflected off the surface dynamically illuminates the underside of the outdoor living area. From this part of the house there is a beautiful southern vista and an intimate northern view of the water landscape.

The configuration of the swimming pool on the southern tip of the site is both functional and aesthetic. Following the natural topography of the site, the pool breaks from the rectangular form of the house and is visually integrated with the landscape. The outermost edge of the pool is masked by cascading water, creating the illusion of extending the landscape of the house into the desert beyond. This effect reinforces the natural form of the ravine, breaks down the boundary between the built and the natural landscape, and continues the exploration of the language of extension.

The legibility of design strategies such as embedding, framing, and extending in Vanishing Rain underscores Hovey's ongoing research and experimentation within his architectural language. Spatial relationships, programmatic distributions, and sensitivity to context are all brought together creating a complex set of experiences within a controlled language of materials and structure.

"I sensed that the mass should be apparent on all elevations, even though the south needed transparency for views. I freed the fireplace from the floor to ceiling glass envelope, creating sheltered outdoor space at both levels."

83

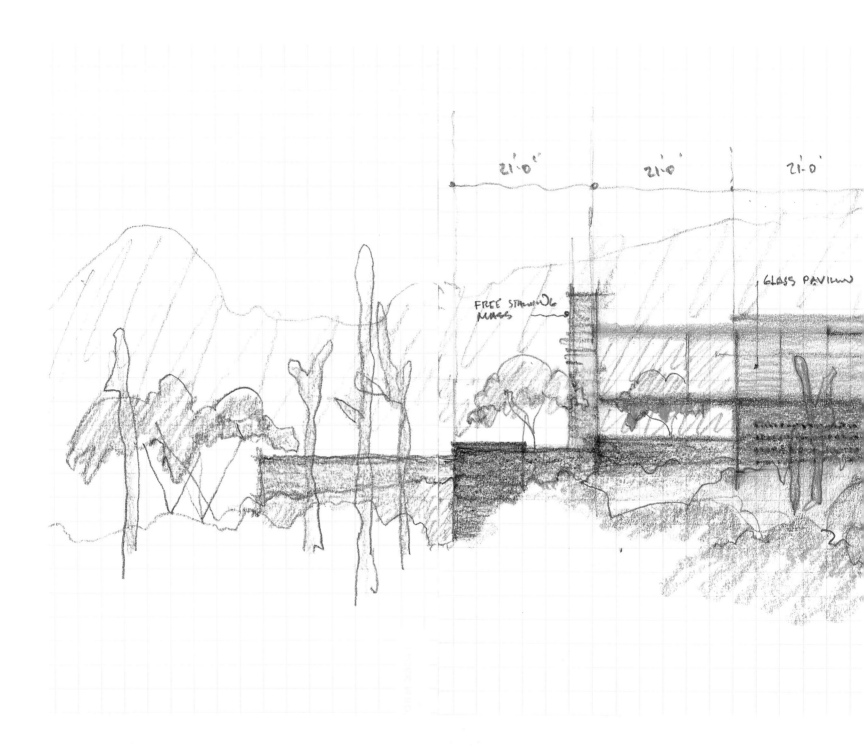

21'-0"   21'-0"   21'-0"

FREE STANDING
MASS

GLASS PAVILION

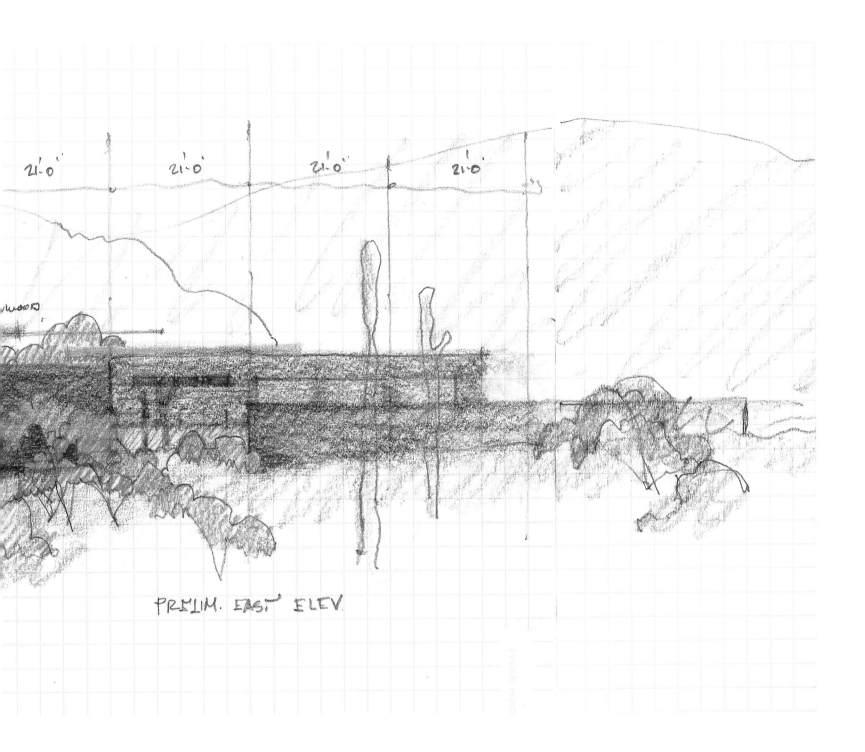

21'-0"   21'-0"   21'-0"   21'-0"

PRELIM. EAST ELEV.

87

Vanishing Rain entry level plan

Vanishing Rain lower level plan

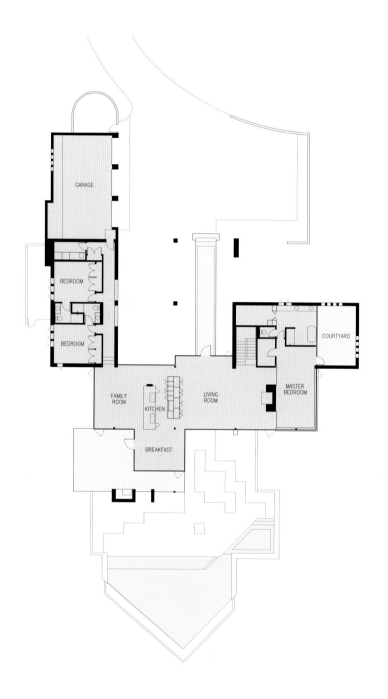

GARAGE

BEDROOM

BEDROOM

FAMILY
ROOM

KITCHEN

LIVING
ROOM

MASTER
BEDROOM

COURTYARD

BREAKFAST

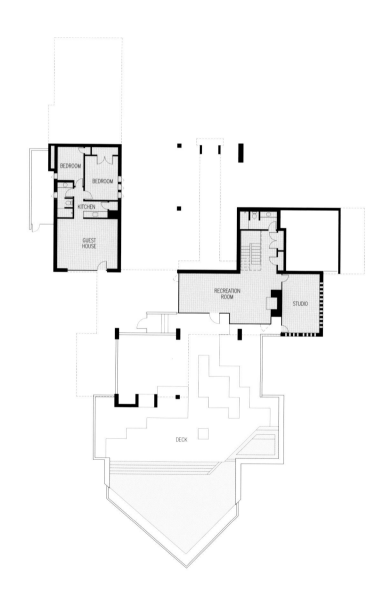

BEDROOM

BEDROOM

KITCHEN

GUEST
HOUSE

RECREATION
ROOM

STUDIO

DECK

10   20   40

shadow caster

2001
Scottsdale, Arizona

"I excavated the driveway to expose the forms of the boulders and to keep the viewers' eye below the roofline on the approach to the house. As a transition between the compacted surface of the courtyard and the severe lines of the house, I introduced a water feature edged with irregular flat stones intended to look like torn watercolor paper."

"This is what I imagined when I saw the site. I was captivated by the concept of the house straddling the mounds on either side with open space underneath."

bridging art and architecture

Cheryl Kent

Shadow Caster does not try to disappear into the desert; rather it looks exactly like the carefully conceived, harmoniously structured intervention it is. Geometry sets the house apart from the soft surrounding hills, but the edges between structure and landscape are blurred by the house's colors—which blend into the desert's pink and red palette—and by the way the house rests in the landscape. Shadow Caster is married to the exotically beautiful Sonoran Desert with an architectural authority.

Hovey chose the community at Desert Mountain for its surpassing beauty and its strict design regulations requiring owners and builders to preserve the desert landscape. The site he selected for Shadow Caster, built himself and his family, is topographically complex. Extremely rugged with slopes angling down in every direction, it presented more challenges than building on level ground. The payoff, however, is substantial. The 7,000-square-foot house has been designed and constructed like a bridge spanning a ravine—now a series of stepped outdoor courtyards—to be anchored at the east and west ends on opposing hills. Because the house has effectively been hoisted to the summit of the site, its views toward Scottsdale are lengthened and dramatized

while the close-up views of the hills and the eccentric vegetation are intact. The twin pull between examining what is near at hand and what is distant is a recurring theme throughout the house and its surroundings.

On the east and west ends of the house, where the exposure to the sun is greatest through the day, the walls are built of insulated masonry. Slow to absorb heat and cold alike, these massive walls help keep the house cool in the day and warm at night. The north and south elevations are glass to take advantage of the views. The way in which the house is used changes with the season. In summer, the shade below the bridge structure makes it possible to be outdoors despite the intense heat. When temperatures are cool, the exposure to the sun on the south terrace extends outdoor use through the winter.

The structure is straightforward with a concrete slab foundation poured directly onto the minimally graded site. Steel beams form the horizontal supports for both the bridge and the roof with enormous cantilevers stretching out as far as 28 feet. Steel grating projecting from the roof provides shading as well as beautiful patterning effects. The vertical load-bearing elements, including the walls and columns, are made of a standard concrete block tinted to match the color of the

desert. The internal face of the block was ground in the factory to reveal the texture of the aggregate. When the house was finished, the outer face of the block was sandblasted to give it the same flat non-reflective quality in sunlight as the desert terrain itself.

The house is laid out like a pinwheel. Spun off the bridge area, where the living and dining spaces are located, are the guesthouse (actually an independent structure connected to the house by a walkway), kitchen, master bedroom and bath, laundry room, and a second bedroom. On the lower level—reached by a spectacular inside stair of individually cantilevered orange-colored steel treads—there is another guest area with a bedroom and bath, a seating area, the courtyard, and a separate small studio. Boundaries between the interior and exterior are dematerialized by the extensive use of glass. Together, multiple openings providing quick access to the outdoors, combined with the need to go outside to reach either the studio or the guesthouse, reinforce a sense of passing through an "invisible curtain"—in Hovey's phrase—as one moves in, out, and through the house. This permeable quality makes the experience of the house inseparable from that of the landscape in which it rests.

The approach along a curving road gradually reveals the house. From this vantage point, the terraced lower level is invisible so the entire structure appears to be a single story hugging the land. Unlike a formal entry where the circulation is scripted, Hovey offers choices. From an outdoor courtyard visitors may descend stairs to the terraced level, the courtyard, and pool

or follow a path leading to the door into the principal living space on the elevated bridge structure. With glass on two sides, the bridge is completely transparent so that, from the entry gate, there are views of the distant hills through the structure. The choices are equally compelling, offering either the long or the close view, selecting between the fine details of exotic plantings and the grandeur of a beckoning vista.

The architect's intention to reduce everything to the minimum is evident throughout the interior. The large planes of glass are unframed and set directly into the routed concrete block walls and the concrete flooring. A concealed glass wall slides out—pulled without effort despite its size—to contain the master bedroom suite. The furnishings throughout the house are, for the most part, classic Modern pieces with simple clean lines.

The exceptions are the pieces from George Nakashima's studio, of which the Hoveys must be among the world's principal collectors. There are stools, a side table, headboards, a sideboard, and a dining table for eight in the house. Each piece is an exploration of the intersection between the organic world and human intervention. Nakashima used the natural form and grain of wood—often leaving gnarled edges as they were—and juxtaposed it with crafted features like straight edges and butterfly joints. As much art as furniture, these pieces assert nothing less than the possibility of man's coexistence with nature. This concept may be precisely what appeals to Hovey about Nakashima's work. For the message implicit in both men's work is essentially the same. With its strong geometry and industrial materials, Hovey's house is frank about its manmade roots while remaining utterly sympathetic to the desert landscape.

Hovey and his wife, Eileen, are serious art collectors, and the works assembled here reinforce the house and Hovey's architectural purpose in different ways. An exuberant wall relief by Frank Stella, with its joyous coloration and sinuous shapes, may appear more like a foil to the geometry and simplicity of the house than an echo of its themes, but architect and artist share fundamental concerns. Both are interested in structure, in contemporary materials and in using color as a means of expression. Stella borrowed a sandwiched aluminum prized for its lightness by the aircraft industry so the piece could be hung. (The relief, which measures nine by ten feet, would have been impossibly heavy otherwise.) The properties of the aluminum, with its industrial connotations and its lovely sheen, are integral to the work, as are the bright colors, which have been applied directly to the aluminum using paint and wax crayons. The placement of the relief energizes the large living area without, in the least, dominating the architecture. Hovey's eloquent rejoinder was to hang the relief above his orange stair.

None of the materials, shapes, or colors Stella used had a place in the world of high art before artists like Stella made room for them. So, too, David Hovey has used compositional devices and materials —steel, glass, concrete block, the cantilever—not usually found in houses. In doing so, he has expanded the architectural vocabulary and made a beautiful house that is right for its time.

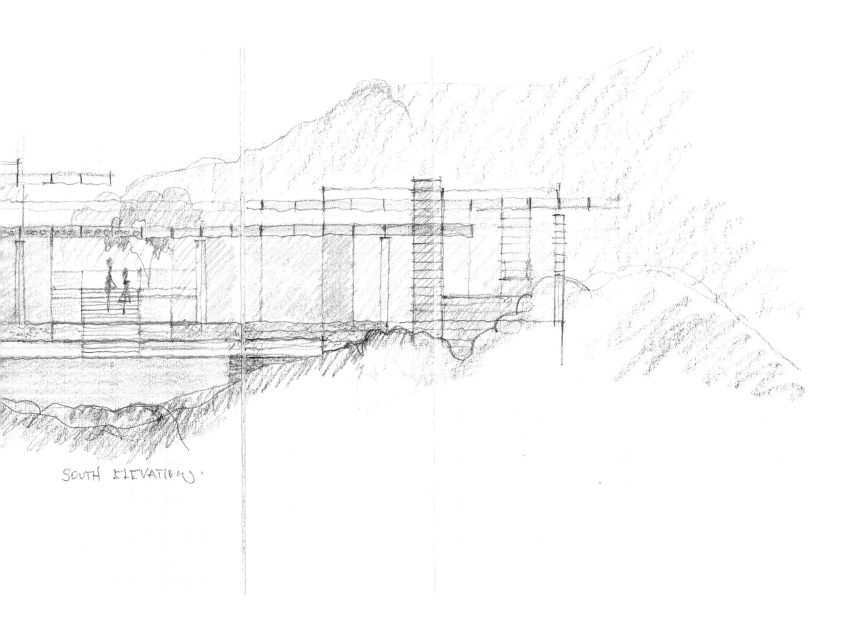

SOUTH ELEVATION

107

"The east and west elevations are more opaque to protect the interior from the morning and afternoon sun. Concrete block was a good, indigenous, modular material. Sandblasting the exterior exposed the rich colors of the aggregate."

Shadow Caster entry level plan

Shadow Caster lower level plan

BEDROOM

BEDROOM

GUEST
HOUSE

GARAGE

BEDROOM

FOYER

LIVING
ROOM

DINING
ROOM

DECK

KITCHEN

MASTER
BEDROOM

FAMILY
ROOM

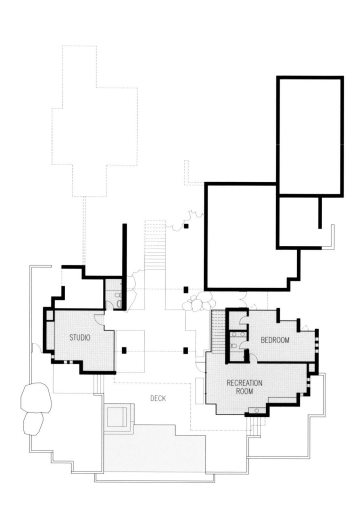

STUDIO

BEDROOM

DECK

RECREATION
ROOM

10   20   40

"Entry, living, and dining are all
contained in one large volume with
a ceiling height of 14 feet. The
intent was to create raw beauty
from total simplicity: one concrete
block exposed inside and out,
a sheet of glass, a metal ceiling,
and a concrete floor."

"Although the house has immense amounts of glass, overhanging roof planes keep the exterior balcony and interior in shadow. These admit shifting light, much like an arbor with sun shining through vines."

"The house at night summarizes
my concept of structure in relation
to function and the aesthetics
of architectural expression."

ravine bluff

1995
Winnetka, Illinois

a machined model of affordable design

Cheryl Kent

David Hovey is an unreformed Modernist, enchanted by technology, beguiled by new materials, and fascinated by the problem of affordable housing. While most architects were embracing historically based styles in the 1980s, Hovey stayed with Modernism out of conviction. Philosophically, he believes technology can provide solutions to housing. Aesthetically, he has a passion for interiors unobstructed by columns and walls, floor-to-ceiling glass, and uncomplicated structural frames that are among the hallmarks of modern architecture.

The home that Hovey created for himself in Winnetka, a Chicago suburb, is a laboratory in which he tests his ideas and indulges his tastes. It is a stunning house, at once industrial in appearance and unaffectedly beautiful. The house reflects Hovey's elegant Modernist sensibility as well as much of what he has learned about building economically.

The house, standing on a 60-foot bluff overlooking Lake Michigan, took only six months to design and build. That kind of fast-tracking is central to Hovey's conception of affordable housing. He uses unconventional materials and building methods to achieve economies that by his estimation reduce the cost of custom design and construction by half and the time for design and construction by as much as two-thirds.

The structural frame was prefabricated in three weeks, and it took just two days to erect with a large crane. It was designed with ease of construction in mind: the simpler the connections joining it, the less time it would take to assemble on site and the greater the savings in manpower and equipment. Construction details affect design considerations in other ways. For example, the span of the house is 35 feet, which corresponds to the maximum length of an object that a flatbed truck can legally carry on an interstate. The stair, with its exceptionally long 20-foot cantilever, was also made off site. It was plugged in after the frame was built and before the flooring was in place. The most labor-intensive component, requiring a full two weeks to attach, was the curtain wall that wraps the entire 8,500-square-foot structure.

More than a year after the house was finished, Hovey added a lower deck to the east side. It, too, was prefabricated and brought in by truck. He plans further alterations, so the house will continue

to change over time. Such an evolution seems appropriate for a building that is assembled as if from Legos.

The British architects Lord Norman Foster and Sir Richard Rogers are among those who share Hovey's interest in buildings with an industrial appearance and a technologically sophisticated edge. But those architects achieve their effects at far greater cost by custom-designing and custom-manufacturing the building components. In contrast, Hovey adapts existing industrial materials to his purposes. In this way he borrows the economies of scale developed for industry and uses them for housing.

The beautiful satin-sheen exterior aluminum panels that shield private areas of Hovey's house from view are a case in point: they were fabricated by a company that manufactures such panels for buses. For the exterior soffit, he used a material that was commonly employed for buried piping. It does not stain, and it has a lovely neutral color and finish. The sparkling mesh on the outside of the garage is fencing pressed into service as a trellis. Indeed as Hovey sees it, his practice of borrowing from industry could make housing for the middle class look more vital and interesting than it does now.

For all the talk of cost cutting, that is not what springs to mind when touring this house. Rather, there is a luxuriousness that comes from the rich appeal of open space and unimpeded views. On approach, the house looks nearly transparent: glimpses of the lake are visible through it. It appears to be two stories tall, but a third story is tucked below on

"In siting the house, I wanted to focus
on the lake but also to set back so
that the view from within was filtered
through trees."

come to being in the storm without getting wet. It is an intimacy with nature that people with load-bearing walls and punched windows will never get.

There is no attempt to disguise or conceal the house on its site. Rather, it seems to spring up from its surroundings. Like the structure of the house, the decks are brilliantly colored, red and bright green, to emphasize the demarcation between the house and its wooded environment.

Indeed, contrast is key to appreciating the house. The rigidity of the steel frame is tempered by color. The bright yellow is the visual equivalent of a laugh. Holes punched into steel beams lighten the weight of the structure without compromising its strength. Handmade wood furniture by George Nakashima softens the architecture. The artwork has a similar impact. A life-size bronze sculpture of a woman by Auguste Rodin is near the center of the floor. This sensuous form, a celebration of the complex curve, stands in contrast to the angular geometry of the architecture. Abstract works by Joan Miro, Alexander Calder, Isamu Noguchi, and others are similarly at home here, neither dominated nor overwhelmed by the house.

Originally published in *The New York Times* July 18, 1999.
Reprinted with permission of the author.

the terraced slope leading down to the lake. The cantilevered stair is visible from outside, as is the jaunty bright-yellow steel frame of the house with punched I-beams spanning the width.

Inside, all the rooms offer views of Lake Michigan to the east. The plan on the first floor is completely open: spaces melt into one another with only the suggestion separation implied by built-in shelving or cabinets and floating walls. The space is not cozy in the conventional sense of that word. There are no chintz-covered window seats beckoning one to come and read Jane Austen, but reading Salman Rushdie's thoroughly contemporary fiction here is a real possibility.

For all its machined elements, the house invites engagement with nature. Watching a storm come over the lake from a steel and glass house is as close as one can

"The interior architecture is minimal:
a yellow structure, a Douglas
fir deck screwed directly to the steel,
and a glass curtain wall hanging
independently on the outside."

Ravine Bluff upper level plan

Ravine Bluff entry level plan

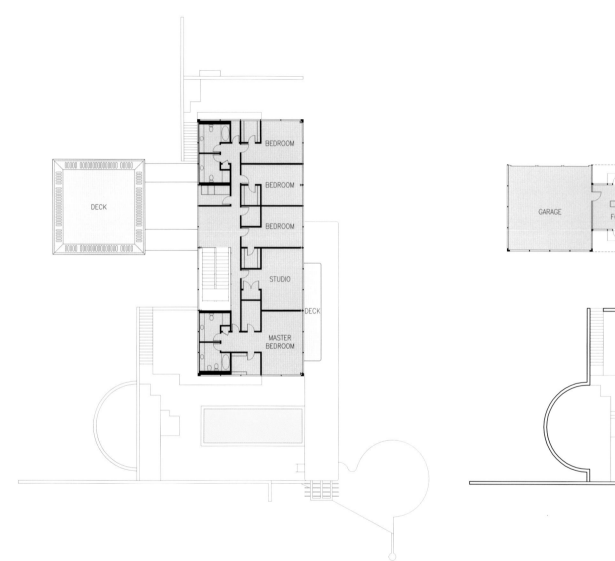

DECK

BEDROOM

BEDROOM

BEDROOM

STUDIO

DECK

MASTER
BEDROOM

KITCHEN

FAMILY
ROOM

GARAGE

FOYER

BREAKFAST

DINING
ROOM

LIBRARY

LIVING
ROOM

DECK

LOWER COURTYARD

LOWER
DECK

10 20 40

1085
RAVINE BLUFF - DECKS.

143

"I envisioned the decks as bold floating
planes, distinctively different in
shape from each other and the house.
The main consideration in detailing
was to minimize foundations on
the slope of the bluff. The yellow strut
prevents tipping; the green supports
the cantilever."

"Although conventional wisdom suggests that architecture should be neutral to best show art, I thought there were other possibilities. Here works by Rodin, Maillol, Moore, Stella, Olitsky, Calder, Miro, Noguchi, and Shapiro seem to make the total visual experience better."

"It was my intention that the clarity of the structure and the methods of construction would not be lost in the completed building. Reduced to its essentials, the house is basically a concrete foundation, a yellow skeleton frame, a white skin curtain wall, and floating horizontal planes stepping down the bluff."

sandy knoll

1984
Homewood, Illinois

ₐ record house

Herbert L. Smith Jr.

It is somehow very appropriate to include this house, with its spare elegance, in this thirtieth issue of *Record Houses*. It tidily crystallizes a number of the evolving aesthetics and concerns of those thirty years: from bright red lally columns to open planning: from "modular coordination" to pre-fab "design-build" concepts. But it is hardly just a case of déjà vu or "historic revivalism" Everything has been carefully rethought, and used to obtain optimum space, timing and costs for this era— all executed with a simple freshness and verve.

The basic program was typical: a young family with a very limited budget, who wanted the most square-footage for their money—including three bedrooms, two baths, and a two-car garage. However, the site they chose—beautifully wooded and about 45 minutes from Chicago— was a small, steeply sloping one with difficult sandy soil conditions. More crucially, they had within three months from the time they contacted architect David Hovey to move from quarters they then occupied.

Though they went to him because they liked a house he had built for himself, Hovey turned out to be an unusually interesting choice. Long interested in industrial techniques, Hovey had previously used some modular ideas in housing. With the short timeframe available to

produce this house, it was a challenge to further explore an aim of prefabricating a basic structure to be erected in one day—and to cut typical red tape and costs of individual houses by combining design and contracting with standard, modular products.

A plan was quickly developed, based on eleven welded-steel modules of 10 by 24 feet—nine feet tall where enclosed— and with all elements selected on a basic two-foot unit. Working drawings were produced in a couple of weeks, permits soon obtained, and a large prefabricator of press-formed steel channels contracted to deliver welded "steel envelopes," with floors and ceilings in place, on eleven semi trucks. With the aid of a crane, they were assembled in one day. As most of the other elements were prefinished, the family enthusiastically moved in at the end of the three months. And for the long range, energy concerns were not forgotten: thermal glass (only one wall, and high strip windows elsewhere, some operable sash) and thick insulation in all the voids.

Reprinted with permission from *Architectural Record*, a division of the McGraw-Hill Companies.

Sandy Knoll plan

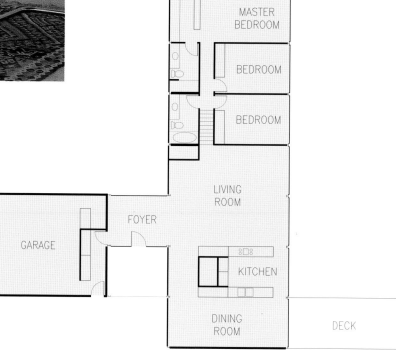

| MASTER BEDROOM |
| BEDROOM |
| BEDROOM |
| LIVING ROOM |
| FOYER |
| GARAGE |
| KITCHEN |
| DINING ROOM |
| DECK |

10   20   40

"Sandy Knoll is a more practical version of my master's thesis project at IIT. The thesis house (above) was based on a single module (21 x 90 x 10 feet) supported on a single column at each end that would have required a Sikorsky sky crane to lift it into place. At Sandy Knoll, the module was designed to fit on a truck and we used a mobile crane."

"This house is better because it steps down the site. The steep slope gave me the opportunity to do something unique, and the use of modular construction preserved the mature trees."

sheridan elm

1982
Winnetka, Illinois

machine meets nature

David Woodhouse

At Sheridan-Elm, Hovey designed a house for himself and his family that develops, almost to exaggeration, the familiar bipolarities of machine-made/natural and rational/romantic, creating an exciting and articulate visual environment defined by their tensions.

The central opposition that Hovey posits is that between the technological and the natural. The house exemplifies the solution of its program within the context of modern technology; design, fabrication, and erection of prefabricated lightweight structural frames, curtain walls, partitions, and mechanical core components are carefully coordinated.

The house is contained in a 30-by-60-foot rectangle divided into five 12-foot transverse bays by its column system, each bay then being further subdivided into four 3-foot transverse sections by the joint system of the house. Longitudinally, the columns are arranged asymmetrically, forming 12-foot and 18-foot bays. The structure consists of slender press-formed steel channel columns that support a ribbed galvanized-steel deck with concrete fill at the second floor and a second deck with rigid insulation at the roof. The ground floor is a concrete slab on grade.

The infilling curtain wall combines large panels of insulated glass and custom prefabricated sandwich panels of unpainted transite exterior panels secured with self-drilling, self-tapping stainless-steel screws, two-inch-thick high performance urethane insulation, and medium density fiberboard interior panels. Both solid and transparent panels are thoughtfully detailed to be directly attached or pocket glazed to the press-formed steel columns, obviating the need for a separate sash system. Because no studs or stiffeners are needed to give rigidity to the solid panels, they can be kept surprisingly thin (less than three inches). Interiors partitions are either medium density fiberboard or gypsum board on steel studs. Most floors are covered with thin industrial carpeting or large no-wax vinyl sheets commonly used for ballet stage floors.

The blue-painted stair provides a dramatic sculptural element separating the central entrance hall from the corner double-height living space. The stair is distinguished by its economical detailing. Its treads, risers, and landings are formed from single sheets of 1/8-inch-thick steel. These sheets are attached along their sides at the break-points to two slender steel rods, forming trussed stringers which, with the addition of two steel suspension rods attached to the ceiling deck, are the stair's only supports. The delicately scaled handrails are also made up of steel rods welded to vertical steel pipes.

"The red joists on the elevations express the difference between the double-height open living room and the two adjacent spaces. The asymmetrical composition of glass rectangles and vertical and horizontal steel is aesthetically more pleasing than a more predictable relationship."

These materials are combined in such a way that each element is particularized and its method of attachment celebrated, while each system forms a well-integrated whole. This approach is reinforced by the color scheme. Only the three primaries are used—all joists are red, accent walls are yellow, and the stair is blue—as a reminder that they form an irreducible kit of parts.

These elements are assembled in an eminently rational way, but with a rationality enlivened by paradox. The house's nominal front and back are really its ends, asymmetrically organized by their steel columnar structures and by their curtain-wall patterns to reflect the private activities that take place behind them. By contrast, the nominal sides (the front and back, in fact) are symmetrically and rather classically organized, with a central entrance emphasized by a latticelike, open joist porte cochere, a brightly colored awning, and a frontal relationship with the public entrance lawn/driveway. The stair, too, offers simultaneous alternate readings. Viewed front-on, its runs seem solid, while from the side they are open and nearly invisible. Finally, the grid itself presents a paradox: a secondary level of directionality, much more subtle than the primary longitudinal/transverse one, is imparted to the structure. This is done by the simple (and, from the technical point of view, quite sensible) device of turning all the open sides of the press-formed steel channels columns and joists in the same direction, thereby making the structural elements look either solid or hollowed, depending on the vantage point of the viewer.

All this technological expression would run some risk of being just another sterile exercise in machine imagery if it were not for the sensitive and powerful way in which the house and its elements are placed within their natural surroundings. The house is surrounded by dense and luxuriant foliage, which acts as a foil to the machine-made aesthetic, humanizing it. On the side where a neighboring house crowds very close, there are low strip windows, which allow a glimpse of the lawn. The solid panels of the curtain wall, the pergola connection to the garage, and the porte cochere will soon be softened by ivy vines. The living room, family room, and master bedroom all have particularly dramatic backdrops of lawn, foliage, or sky. This opposition of the machine-made to the natural is also emphasized by the house's interior furnishings. Some pieces, modern classics of the tubular steel and leather variety, recede into the background. The majority, however, are handcrafted natural wood pieces by George Nakashima, flamboyant and expressionistic, glorifying even the flaws in the wood. All this comes together to create a powerful tension between these two worlds.

The rational/romantic bipolarity is explored more tentatively than the machine-made/natural. Romantic elements include the sweeping stairway, the blue-and-white striped awning, and (eventually) ivy-covered pergolas. These reminders of other worlds create their own tensions with the overall technological imagery of the house and are all the stronger for ironically being executed by modern technological means.

Originally published in *Progressive Architecture*, July 1983.
Reprinted with permission of the author.

Sheridan Elm upper level plan

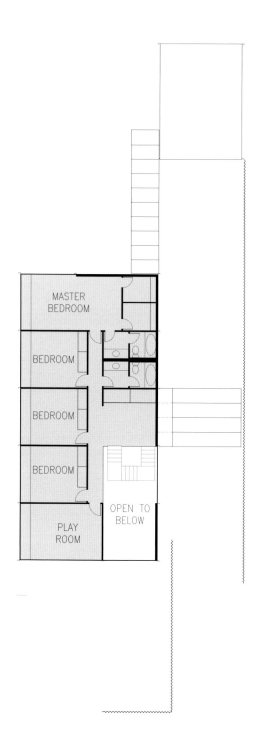

MASTER
BEDROOM

BEDROOM

BEDROOM

BEDROOM

PLAY
ROOM

OPEN TO
BELOW

Sheridan Elm entry level plan

© Yoshio Takase

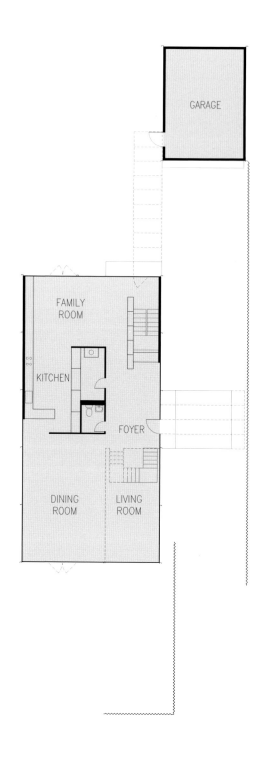

GARAGE

FAMILY
ROOM

KITCHEN

FOYER

DINING
ROOM

LIVING
ROOM

10   20   40

© Yoshio Takase

174

"This is a dynamic space with the blue stair as sculpture. The bold colors were selected to give a sense of warmth and fantasy to a basically industrial palette of materials."

optima

Founded 1978
Glencoe, Illinois
Phoenix, Arizona

david hovey: an uncommon architect

Cheryl Kent

Like all architects, David Hovey wants to see his work built. Unlike almost all architects, he has found a way to do it without clients, maintaining complete control of project. He has made his own way by combining design, construction, and development in Optima, the office he founded in 1978, and by focusing almost exclusively on multi-family housing. It was Hovey's ambition to have his own company and to design significant contemporary housing during his days in graduate school in the late 1960s; at that time, he believed he would build housing from a factory using prefabrication techniques. As an ideal he looked to Jean Prouvé, who designed and fabricated his structurally pure and prescient furniture and buildings out of his own shop. When pure prefabrication proved impracticable, Hovey focused on honing efficient construction techniques, using inexpensive industrial processes and unusual materials that would still allow him to build high-quality housing economically. In doing so, he has explored the most fundamental ways of integrating materials and systems. "If I can do it with one material, that's better than two. If I can do it with two, it's better than three," Hovey says.

Hovey studied at the Illinois Institute of Technology where the architecture program was founded by Mies van der Rohe. But he is more likely to quote Vitruvius's famous dictum of "firmness, commodity, and delight" as his guiding principle than he is to quote Mies. Structure, function, and beauty are the three measures by which he judges his work. Unlike Mies, the purist, Hovey is willing to be flexible to achieve all three. "There is more than one solution to every problem," he says.

It would be difficult to imagine a worse time than the late 1970s to take the step Hovey did. Interest rates were climbing toward the 20 percent high they would reach a few years later. In addition, Hovey's taste for contemporary structurally expressive architecture was at odds with the postmodern style then in vogue. If that was not enough, the idea that architects could meaningfully contribute to housing on an urban-planning scale went down with Pruitt-Igoe in 1972, according to conventional interpretation. At the domestic scale, architects' involvement in housing had ended by 1962, according to Esther McCoy, who wrote, famously, about the Case Study houses.

The idea of combining construction and design was considered heretical among architects, raising questions about potential conflicts. Hovey turned aside the criticism. He had become acutely aware of the wasted time and effort in the traditional relationships between architect, client, and contractor. As a result, he was convinced that what he was doing was the only way to lower the costs of building housing, and he felt it was a very good way to control the architectural integrity of a project.

Optima Views, 2002

"This design captures the best views for every residence, and each elevation is different. One is flat with a tier of recessed terraces, the second has louvers to shield the interiors from the sun, the third is faceted to provide views of the lake, and the fourth is like a needlepoint because of its relationship to the street."

Hovey has not given up on the substance of the ideal shaped in postwar America: that good, tastefully designed, inventive and, above all, contemporary architecture can and should shelter American families. The ideal came closest to realization in the California Case Study houses designed by the likes of Richard Neutra, Charles Eames, and Raphael Soriano, who like Hovey, also managed his own construction. These elegant, ultramodern houses were believed at the time to be the models for what would become available to everyone. Instead, builders and developers took over the housing market on the powerful basis of the economies they were able to offer and architects were, for the most part, marginalized.

With the combined disciplines in his office, Hovey is able to compete with builders and developers on economics. More important, because he is a gifted architect, he beats them soundly on design. As a developer, Hovey adheres to standards of responsible design. His multi-family work is built in communities, typically in-fill projects that fortify what exists rather than contributing to sprawl. In downtown Phoenix, where the urban center desperately needs definition and consolidation, the 230-unit Optima Biltmore Towers is just getting underway. He is able to make all this work because he sees architecture and business as two factors in a balanced equation.

Hovey faces the same constraints as other developers: legitimate community scrutiny and, interestingly enough, as a kind of blowback from Modernism's excesses, community suspicion. Design guidelines are now common in suburbs and developments, and zoning variances are not easy

Optima Views

to come by. Hovey finds himself arguing before hostile village boards, design review committees, and community groups about the rightness of his vision. He is in the curious position of defending his work as a conscientious architect before a community suspicious of developers.

By controlling design, development, and construction, Hovey has been able to shift the emphasis in market housing to architecture from economics. It is ironic that from a position once considered a potential breach of ethics, Hovey has leveraged a position to advance architecture as well as the quality of the building stock. Today, major architectural commissions are largely confined to institutional and public projects—university buildings, museums, courthouses, and the like. Only a small number of architects have the opportunity to generate such designs, and, sadly, relatively few citizens are able to enjoy their work. That makes Hovey's achievement all the more impressive because, against considerable and growing odds, he is improving the quality of the everyday built world. Over the past twenty-five years, Optima has completed 30 projects, creating more than 3,000 units of well-designed housing occupied by thousands of people and seen by more every day.

Hovey has built only seven single-family houses, but he has used them to test design ideas that find application in his large-scale work. In that respect, the houses in this book are at once exceptional and absolutely representative of his work. As a subset in a larger portfolio, the houses exhibit the design sensibility, planning, and some of the details characteristic of the larger projects. In contrast to his

multi-family work, Hovey's houses are more personal, more revealing of his own architectural tastes. Nowhere is this more true than in the houses Hovey has designed in the Chicago area. Unconstrained by market concerns, Hovey was completely free to experiment. Given that opportunity, he chose to get as close to approximating prefabrication as he could by exploiting industrial capabilities.

The first of these, Sheridan-Elm, is a super lightweight two-story steel-framed house with a combination of infill glass and solid panels. The elegant three-turn stair, which seems to hang in space, was made of continuous press-formed, 10-gauge steel plates. Nearly everything that went into the construction was prefabricated off-site

Hyde Park, 1978

"As a young architect, I wanted to control the whole building process— buy the land, design and construct the buildings, and market and manage them. The goal was to create architecturally significant buildings of high quality and careful attention to detail. Hyde Park was our first venture —a complex of six town houses."

187

840 Michigan Avenue, 1985

"Located on a prominent urban site, this complex consists of 16 town houses with private gardens and 8 penthouses with private terraces. At the center is a landscaped courtyard. Bridges fabricated of aluminum gratings allow sunlight to penetrate; at night, the channel-glass stair enclosures become giant lanterns to light the space."

by industrial manufacturers—most unrelated to the housing industry—at very little cost in order to meet a tight budget. The idea was to go directly to the shop, skip the middleman, and specify things that were simple, giving precise directions so the fabricator had no guesswork.

Hovey accepted the commission for Sandy Knoll because he thought he could develop what he had done at Sheridan-Elm. Again, using press-formed steel, Hovey designed eleven modules, each 10 x 10 x 20 feet, with ceilings and floors attached. These were to be trucked to the site and bolted into place forming a three-bedroom house with an attached garage. The assembly took just one day. The house steps down, following the steep slope of the site and demonstrating as it does so, the adaptability of the modular solution. It may seem ironic that Hovey's only commissioned house, and one of his earliest independent projects, was also his purest experiment in prefabrication—a one-off that could conceivably have been ramped up to roll off an assembly line in multiples of thousands to house middle-class America. Since that was not going to happen, Hovey applied what he learned to the multi-family projects.

In 1985, he designed and developed 840 Michigan, a 24-unit infill complex, with a hybrid structure of brick bearing walls, precast concrete floors, and exposed steel. A courtyard separates the units, 12 to each side, and serves as entryway. He had intended to use manufactured preformed concrete throughout, a good material candidate for prefabrication that he was anxious to try. To his frustration, he found the precast would be more costly than brick— what he had once called "an archaic material." So, as he had before, Hovey turned to custom steel fabrication, and his own ingenuity. The court stairways leading to the penthouses glass are similar, if

less complex, than those Hovey installed in Sheridan-Elm. The experimental window detail he had used there had worked and was simple and elegant. He used it again, placing the glass directly in the pocket of the exterior steel frame and caulking it in place. The opaque panels at Sheridan-Elm reappear here as fencing. Construction took only one year, demonstrating Hovey's point that the economies in combining disciplines were manifested in more ways than one.

Hovey had his first chance to use precast concrete as both structural and cladding material at Optima Center, a seven-story, mixed-use residential project in suburban Chicago. The materials permitted rapid construction in winter conditions. A five-story steel-and-glass elevator core was prefabricated and installed in one day. At the 1990 North Pointe project, Hovey used the same precast as a cladding in a horizontal three- and four-story arrangement. The site was triangular, an abandoned factory at the edge of an upscale suburb. Hovey built 126 town houses and condominiums, bringing all the units out to the edge of the site and opening the center for a common space. For the community, the project replaced the void with a handsome wall of residences.

The 10-story condominium at 1618 Sheridan demonstrates Hovey's conviction that the exterior of a building reflect the interior plan. Using a combination of green glass, metal louvers, and granite, Hovey created individual elevations reflecting the functions, rooms, and views from within.

Optima Center, 1988

"Mixed-use can provide vitality. This seven-story building combines retail shops at grade with three stories of office space topped by three stories of apartments. A four-story glass atrium serves as a communal area connecting all three functions."

Opposite: North Pointe

At Ravine Bluff, his home in Winnetka, Illinois, completed in 1995, Hovey revisited the themes introduced in Sheridan-Elm, pushing the experiment a little further. The house has a simple laser-cut steel frame with a 35-foot clear span. It is painted a brilliant yellow and sheathed with a standard glass curtain wall in a minimal white frame. Magnificently sited 60 feet above Lake Michigan, the house achieves a unity with the landscape partly through its near complete transparency. In its unaffected, straightforward what-you-see-is-what-you-get jaunty beauty, the influence of Prouvé is evident. The architectural and structural flourishes are called out in primary colors. The De Stijl palette is especially convincing in the winter and fall when the light is steeply angled and takes on a particular sharpness and clarity. As he has elsewhere, Hovey adapted materials from industries unrelated to housing, borrowing what others have invested in research and development and applying it to his own uses. This house has the assurance and joy of a good architect unleashed, who knows what he is doing and for whom he is doing it.

Hovey says that one reason he built Ravine Bluff was that he was feeling the need for a challenge. Indeed, the house seemed to rejuvenate him. A series of innovative multi-family projects followed in quick succession over the next several years: Michigan Place, Optima Towers, and Optima Views among them. Michigan Place was intended to attract middle-class buyers to an underdeveloped area known as the Gap with high-quality housing. Hovey built 120 units with two seven-story condominium buildings at the north end of the one-block site and town houses to the south allowing sunlight to penetrate throughout. The buildings are all pushed to the edge of the site, strengthening the streetwall, and leaving

the center as an open courtyard. The condominiums are simple, arresting buildings, handsomely proportioned, built of concrete and clad with a framed glass curtain wall. Meaningful architectural details that subtly improve the quality of the entire development have been included, such as the bridge above the courtyard entry, which quietly creates a sense of enclosure without making a barrier. This is the generous, humanizing gesture a good architect makes, and it matters.

Optima Towers and Optima Views in Evanston share the challenge of a difficult site and ingenious responses. The Towers site is adjacent to a small historic building on one side and follows a long angled street on the other. Hovey made the most of what he had, stepping the building on the angled side to catch light and views while creating a lively facade. Zoning called for setbacks, so Hovey gave them a modern interpretation, stepping the building back above the retail level for outdoor, green roof terraces. Train lines run on two sides of the nearly triangular Views site. Hovey took the building up—at 28 stories it is the tallest in town—to take advantage of the views. Its dynamic form is driven by views as well: the faceted side opens to Lake Michigan and the opposite flat elevation looks straight to Chicago. This is Hovey's boldest multi-family building and it is very assured.

During this period, Hovey became interested in building outside Chicago, in a climate and landscape that would require new architectural solutions. Out of this came the four Arizona houses and the Biltmore. Collectively, the scale of these projects signal a point in Hovey's career when he and his firm have achieved the reputation and financial stability allowing him to undertake more than one project at a time and to press harder than ever for contemporary architectural solutions.

North Pointe, 1990

"Because the site was on the perimeter of the community and surrounded by busy streets, I decided to create a sense of place by designing an inner park and lake behind a continuous building that followed the irregular outline of the site. The exterior is principally precast concrete with some glass block at the lower-level parking area."

1618 Sheridan Road, 1992

"This mid-rise building accommodates
only one residence per floor, a
configuration that allows multiple functions
to be expressed on the elevations—
stairs as a sheer wall, mechanical rooms
as louvers—rather than the more
typical organization of locating the
principal rooms at the perimeter behind
floor to ceiling glass. Bay windows
squeeze every last square foot out of the
footprint and huge prefabricated
balconies provide outdoor living space."

When Hovey undertook the single-family speculative luxury homes in Arizona, he seems to have picked the toughest sites he could find. Each of them is elevated and topographically complex; they have wonderful views, but he may like them because they drive him to come up with the most innovative architectural solutions. Many architects talk about the inspiration they get in the give-and-take relationship with clients; Hovey seems to get this from solitary reflection and site conditions.

What is different about these houses from his Midwest work? Everything and nothing. He surely continues to use houses as a way to experiment. As he did at Ravine Bluff, he has used a 7 x 7-foot module, but in Arizona he has more fully exploited its elastic possibilities, using it to create far more complex and layered plans. He has not changed his palette of materials greatly. Steel is still a prominent feature, less evident as a frame than in great cantilevers. The industrial steel grating Hovey has used for decking in Illinois has become a shading device in Arizona. Hovey has always been conscientious about including landscaped areas in his projects, but he seems to have gained a new confidence in Arizona where the relationship between house and landscape is more completely integrated than ever. Each house has its own character, but they share a great deal—the same programs and similarly rugged site. Architectural devices recur in each, terracing and bridging most conspicuously.

Shadow Caster —the first to be completed—is painted steel, glass, and concrete block. The structure is exposed and the materials are neither conventional nor luxurious although the surpassing impression

is surely elegant. A 28-foot cantilever hung off a 21-foot bay is flamboyantly daring although its expression in the house is subtle, more the architect's private challenge to himself. The orange stair, with individually cantilevered treads that spring slightly at each step, is conspicuously wonderful. Straddling a shallow ravine, the house most resembles a great bridge with the principal living space occupying the central span.

Cloud Chaser's essential impression is quite different. This house seems to levitate above the slope. The central space is like an asymmetrical glass box suspended in air. At a critical moment, Hovey enhanced the impression by reducing a column to a thin steel member and then to mere glass where a butt-glazed corner offers a view of distant mountains. Making the structure dematerialize and then nearly disappear gives the illusion of movement as though the room were gliding toward the mountain. It is amazing. It also demonstrates an essential point about Hovey's approach to architecture: he does not insist on architectural purity if the tradeoff is worth it. In this case, he willingly sacrificed expression of his 21 x 21-foot bay for a dramatic spatial instant. Like his willingness to experiment, his flexibility is essential to achieving his best work.

From the east, Sterling Ridge offers massive concrete walls with deeply embedded windows. The house's character changes on the southwest facade where there is floor-to-ceiling glass and balconies sheltered by great steel overhangs. As he did at Cloud Chaser, Hovey has introduced audacious structural moves at Sterling Ridge. Here, a massive 42-foot cantilever —partly compensated by a horizontal tension rod—on the first level balcony eliminated the need for two columns that would have obstructed views. For the first

time, Hovey is incorporating solar energy, and he is allowing the glass-gridded panels to speak for themselves as roof and shading components. The interior is among the most interesting of all the Arizona houses. It has a great double-height space which is a highly active, changing volume, animated by two great steel stairs and an overhanging study.

Hovey's future multi-family projects promise to be all the more interesting for the experiments of the Arizona houses. We are lucky for it. Few may be able to enjoy houses such as these, but many enjoy living in the multi-family projects Hovey has built. When Hovey turns to condominiums, town houses and the like, he elevates a building type that developers and builders had taken away from architects. In doing so, he has restored dignity to the world of market housing and to those who purchase and inhabit it.

Michigan Place, 2000

"This complex integrates historic structures and acknowledges the Miesian campus of IIT across the street. Two multi-faceted towers define the north end of the site and allow maximum sun exposure for the three-story town houses to the south. A grand entrance, centered on a historic church, leads into a landscaped green roofing system over the underground parking area."

Optima Towers, 2001

"The sculptural composition of this building and the orientation of its spaces solved the challenge of a trapezoidal site formed by the intersection of three streets. A landscaped courtyard between the Towers and the adjacent historic building provides a natural separation between the residential entry and the streetfront retail shops. Shimmering green glass and bright orange perforated steel balconies relieve the monochromatic materials of the surrounding buildings."

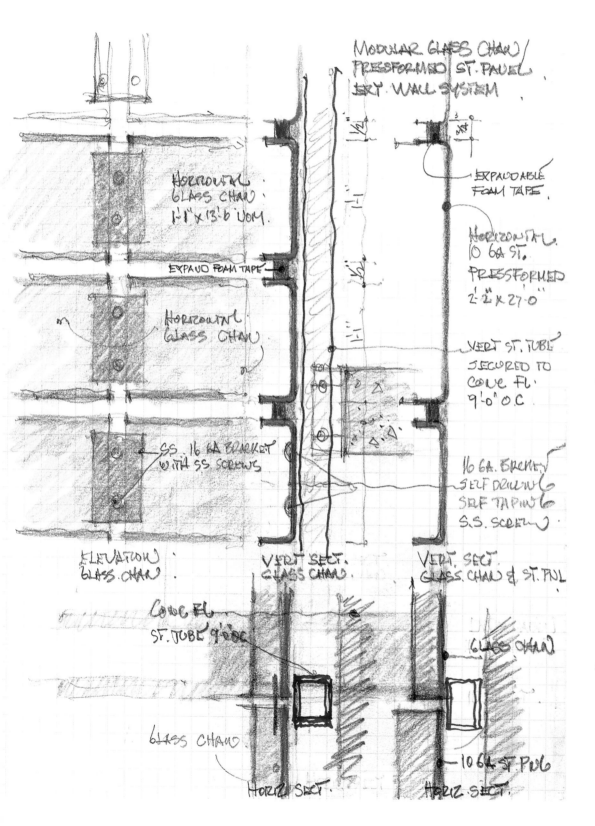

Optima Biltmore, 2004

"The exterior wall of this project in Arizona relies on a kit of parts: metal curtain wall components, green solex glass, translucent channel glass, perforated sunshades, expanded metal screens, extruded aluminum muntins to define recessed terraces, pressformed aluminum slab wrap, and mechanical louvers."

Opposite:
Optima Horizons, 2003

"I was inspired by Jean Prouvé and his idea that buildings should be prefabricated using the most advanced materials and techniques available to all industries. I believe this is the only way to meet today's housing production requirements."

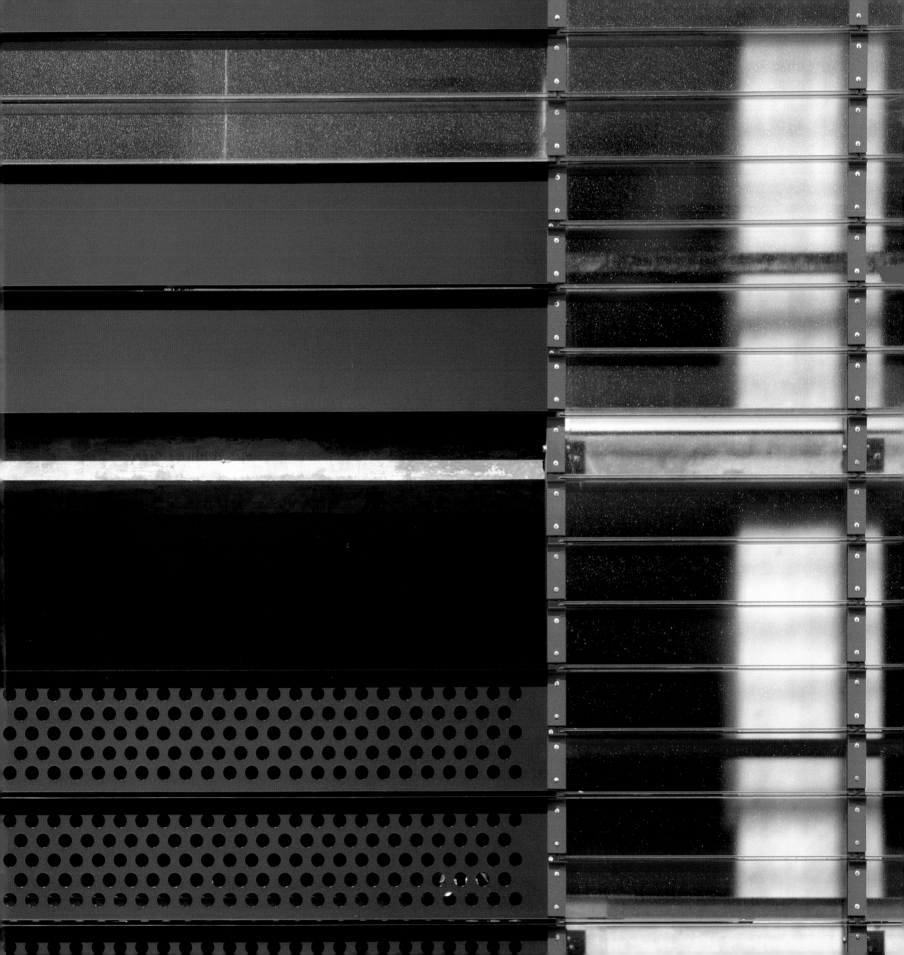

Optima Camelview Village, 2005

"Because every residence has its own outdoor roof terrace to take advantage of the desert climate, the buildings merge as expanding and subsiding pyramids with provocative, positive, and negative space."

PARKING

Acknowledgments

I am deeply indebted to Arthur S. Takeuchi for his mentoring and support of the concept of architect, contractor, and developer that he introduced to me as his student at the Illinois Institute of Technology. Eileen Sheehan Hovey and I started Optima, and she has been responsible for marketing and sales since 1978. Although not an architect, she has been instrumental in the success of the company including encouraging contemporary design.

Tod Desmarais has been with Optima since 1996 and assists me with design and development, while TJ Lenick has specialized in construction and contract administration since 1984. Jennifer Oppenheimer oversees all accounting and financial functions. Todd Kuhlman aided in the design and construction of our recent single-family dwellings.

The following Senior Associates have also contributed significantly on our projects: Mike Schwerzler, Matt Cison, Karl Schneider, Lynn Horton, Tim Pruis, Roman Wachula, and Bill Byrne. Others who have contributed: Efrain Banda, Peter Forester, David Hovey Jr., Chris Karidis, Rebecca Mikolajczyk, Mark Riehle, Jay Shin, Eugene Wesolowski, Rene Garcia, Gene Szmauz, Kathy Zaczynski, Stacey Jahnke, Isabel Carver, Morris Green, Carole Herzog, and Patricia Sullivan.

Structural engineering, which is so inherent to our design, has been admirably handled by Ritweger & Tokay, Inc. and Robert Miller & Associates in our early projects and Thornton Thomasetti in recent years. Mark Landa & Associates helped with Sterling Ridge and Vanishing Rain; ELN, Inc., Ravine Bluff.

Attorneys who have been helpful throughout the years are Phillip Gordon, Alexandra R. Cole, Jordan Peters, Bruce Balonick, and John Murphey. Accounting service on all projects since 1978: Harvey Wineberg, Steve Lewis, and Michael Shain.

Cheryl Kent's development of the book has been invaluable. Robert Jensen has made a key contribution with his creative, artistic, and intellectual input. Elizabeth White helped significantly with coordination and editing throughout the book.

Biography

David Hovey was awarded both his Bachelor of Architecture and Master of Science in Architecture by the Illinois Institute of Technology (IIT), completing his studies in 1970. In 1971 he went to work for Arthur S. Takeuchi, the architect who advised him on his thesis. In 1974, he moved to C.F. Murphy Associates (now Murphy/Jahn), and worked on many of the firm's award-winning projects of that era. In 1978 he founded Optima, with the intention of acting as designer, developer and builder of multi-family housing projects. In the same year, he returned to the architecture program at IIT as an associate professor, a position he continues to hold today. Since Optima's founding, the company has completed more than 30 projects and won 17 design awards. Hovey was named a Fellow of the American Institute of Architects in 1992. His work has been widely published and included in numerous architecture exhibitions. Hovey was born in Wellington, New Zealand in 1944 and moved to the United States at the age of 15.